Hey Alyssa,
Happy 13th Birthday!
Best Girlfriend forever,
hope you enjoy the book!
Totally Best
Friends Forever ↑ it's a
& Ever! summary
of our friendship
paula Deroutka (sort of)

FABULOUS FRIENDS

04 05 06 07 08 WKT 10 9 8 7 6 5 4 3 2

ISBN: 0-7407-4182-9
Library of Congress Control Number: 2003113279

ATTENTION: SCHOOLS AND BUSINESSES

Andrews McMeel books are available at quantity discounts with bulk purchase for educational, business, or sales promotional use. For information, please write to: Special Sales Department, Andrews McMeel Publishing, 4520 Main Street, Kansas City, Missouri 64111.

FABULOUS FRIENDS

A Celebration of Girlfriendship

Gail Goodwin

text by P. L. Stein

**Andrews McMeel
Publishing**

Kansas City

AH, GIRLFRIENDS.

They make the good times
great and the great times
FABULOUS.

After all, who better to **PRIMP** with,

GIGGLE WITH,

and, of course,
GOSSIP with?

When we're out
shopping for the world's
greatest sale, we always remember
that a good friend is the

ULTIMATE
FIND,

even better than
a two-for-one
SHOE SALE.

Girlfriends take you beyond cool

into a world that's hot hot hot!

Furthermore, girlfriend, you are **GRACEFUL**, **CHARMING**, and tu-tu **WONDERFUL**,

perfectly
ANGELIC,

REALLY QUITE TALENTED (that's what all the hoopla is about).

and just a
PRINCESS
of a person.

When it's time to cut loose, there's nothing like heading out together on

THE ULTIMATE ROAD TRIP.

And wherever we go,
we dive right in.

There's always a
SHOPPING SPREE
to make us feel free.

Sometimes, though, it's nice to just stay in and talk about trivial stuff.

LIKE HOW
THE GUYS
ADORE US,

IDOLIZE US,

WORSHIP US.

IT'S
EASY
TO SEE
WHY.

and make us feel
like we can be
anything we want.

HOWEVER
CRAZY THAT
MAY BE.

It's nice to gather
the girls for some serious
pampering, from eyes
and nose

to fingers and toes

to some trés chi-chi clothes!

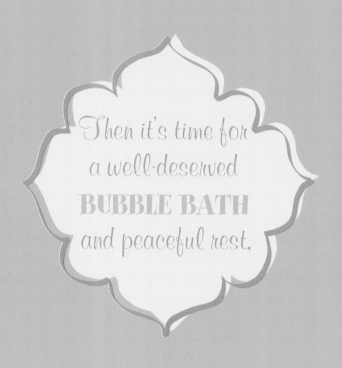

Then it's time for
a well-deserved
BUBBLE BATH
and peaceful rest,

GIRL STYLE!

Girlfriends are always there
when you need a helping hand

or a little lift,

and if there's ever a difference of opinion, they're really good at making up.

Girlfriends help us see things in a whole new way. **THEY HELP US BLOOM**

AND GROW

and become who we were meant to be—
BEAUTIFUL inside and out.

Sure, girls are sugar and spice and everything nice,

but gal pals are so much more. Together we are

ENTREPRENEURIAL,

Lemonade
5¢

TALENTED,

NURTURING,

and as loyal as any
sister ever could be. But
certainly one of the best
things about us is:

When it comes
right down to it,

nobody does it
BETTER

than your best
GAL PAL.

Amazing,
silly,
brilliant,
adorable,
hilarious,
stupendous
GIRLFRIENDS–

SIMPLY
PRICELESS.